My Family at Work

My Uncle Owns a Deli

By Sarah Hughes

Children's Press
A Division of Scholastic Inc.
New York / Toronto / London / Auckland / Sydney
Mexico City / New Delhi / Hong Kong
Danbury, Connecticut

Thanks to La Cucina and Market, Media, PA

Photo Credits: Cover and all photos by Maura Boruchow
Contributing Editors: Jeri Cipriano, Jennifer Silate
Book Design: Victoria Johnson

Visit Children's Press on the Internet at:
http://publishing.grolier.com

Library of Congress Cataloging-in-Publication Data

Hughes, Sarah, 1964-
 My uncle owns a deli / by Sarah Hughes.
    p. cm. -- (My family at work)
   ISBN 0-516-23182-0 (lib. bdg.) -- ISBN 0-516-29578-0 (pbk.)
 1. Restaurants--Vocational guidance--Juvenile literature. 2.
Delicatessens--Juvenile literature. [1. Delicatessens. 2.
Restaurants--Employees. 3. Occupations.]   I. Title.
  TX911.3.V62 H84 2001
  647.95--dc21

                                              00-065763

Contents

Hi, my name is Bob.

This is my **Uncle** Frank.

ORDER HERE
GRAZER
prosciutto w/fresh mozzarella or sharp provolone, roasted peppers or hot peppers & extra virgin oil..............$4.75
DONATA
sopressata, mortadella, sharp provolone, roasted peppers, tomato, lettuce, & olive oil..........$4.75
CAPO
prosciutto, sopressata, sharp provolone & marinated broccoli rabe..........$4.75
Chicken parmigiana..........$4.99
HOAGIES
Gift Certificates
PICKLES

Uncle Frank owns a **deli**.

I like to help him.

We open early.

We make sure everything
is ready.

9

Mr. Smith is here.

He wants a **sandwich**.

I hand it to him.

11

Mrs. Hunt and Lisa come in.

Mrs. Hunt wants a sandwich.

I put it in a bag for her.

13

Uncle Frank **baked** bread.

He puts the bread on the shelf.

Uncle Frank cooked meatballs.

He takes them out of the oven.

Uncle Frank is a great cook!

He makes food for a
big party.

Uncle Frank likes to cook for **neighbors** and friends.

I like to eat what he makes.

New Words

baked (**baykd**) cooked in an oven

deli (**dehl**-ee) a store that sells foods,
   such as cooked meats and cheeses

neighbors (**nay**-buhrz) people who live
   near others

sandwich (**sand**-wihch) food eaten between
   two pieces of bread

uncle (**uhng**-kuhl) the brother of your
   mother or father

To Find Out More

Books
A Busy Day at Mr. Kang's Grocery Store
by Christine Osinski
Children's Press

Do the Doors Open by Magic?
and Other Supermarket Questions
by Catherine Ripley
Owl Communications

Web Site
Zoey's Deli and Bakery
www.zoeys.com
This Web site has games, recipes, and a picture
of a real deli.

Index

About the Author

Sarah Hughes is from New York City and taught school for twelve years. She is now writing and editing children's books. In her free time she enjoys running and riding her bike.

Reading Consultants

Kris Flynn, Coordinator, Small School District Literacy, The San Diego County Office of Education

Shelly Forys, Certified Reading Recovery Specialist, W.J. Zahnow Elementary School, Waterloo, IL

Sue McAdams, Certified Reading Recovery Specialist and Literary Consultant, Dallas, TX